Praying in the Moment

REFLECTIONS ON THE ELECTION OF PRESIDENT BARACK OBAMA

REPORTED BY SHAUNA JAMIESON CARTY

iUniverse, Inc.
Bloomington

Praying in the Moment
Reflections on the Election of President Barack Obama

iUniverse books may be ordered through booksellers or by contacting:

iUniverse
1663 Liberty Drive
Bloomington, IN 47403
www.iuniverse.com
1-800-Authors (1-800-288-4677)

ISBN: 978-1-4620-0237-5 (pbk)
ISBN: 978-1-4620-0238-2 (ebk)

Printed in the United States of America

iUniverse rev. date: 05/16/2011

"Honor your father and mother," which is the first commandment with promise: that it may be well with you and you may live long on the earth. (Ephesians 6:2-3)

Then He (Jesus) spoke a parable to them, that men always ought to pray and not lose heart. (Luke 18:1)

Contents

Preface

In the words of the legendary hymn, we have indeed come this far by faith, leaning on the Lord and trusting in His Holy Word. ***Praying in the Moment*** is a series of reflections that capture the heartfelt emotions that the election of the first African American President of the United States evoked in Americans who have lived through segregation, lynching, and discrimination, and thought they would never live to see the day... Their message to today's youth is to build on the foundation that has been handed to them: have faith in God; study hard; advance academically and professionally. Don't tear down their communities. Don't murder their brothers and sisters.

The series was first published under the title "Election Reflections" in weekly segments and distributed among the congregation at Second Baptist Church in Roselle, New Jersey. This historically black church celebrated its one hundred and eighteenth anniversary in 2008, the year President Barack Obama made history. Reverend James E. Moore, Sr., Pastor of Second Baptist Church suggested interviews with the oldest members of the church in response to Mrs. Shauna Jamieson Carty's request to conduct interviews. Neither one of them anticipated that the stories would so candidly reflect the progress in race relations in the United States of America.

The first eight reflections were reported by Mrs. Jamieson Carty, a journalist and church member, based on her interviews with senior citizens. The ninth reflection provides an excerpt from the diary of Ms. Jennifer Jones, a Ph.D. candidate and church member, who attended the inauguration. The final reflection is a three-part entry by some of the youngest church members who captured their feelings in letters to the president and an essay.

Rev. James Moore, Jr., the pastor's son, made the entire series accessible to readers around the world when he posted the stories on the church's website at secondbaptistroselle. org. Ms. Kareen Nazaire served as part of the web team.

The "Election Reflections" series caught the attention of a *New York Times* reporter who covered it in an article that was published in the Sunday paper two days before Inauguration Day—one day before the observation of Rev. Dr. Martin Luther King, Jr.'s birthday.

Readers responded with an interest in obtaining a book that would permanently capture these stories, and the faces of the people who lived them. After much prayer and persistence that request has now been fulfilled. Praise the Lord! Hallelujah! Thank you, Jesus!

Enjoy.

Acknowledgements

On the night of the election, I sat in my bedroom watching the television news reports. History was being made. The nation was bringing to pass that which was once unthinkable, and I wanted to play a role in reporting it.

All my formal education culminated in my receiving a Master's degree from the journalism school at Columbia University. My newspaper reporting experience peaked at Y2K. Eight years later, I had become fulfilled with a more domestic role, serving as helpmeet to my husband and primary caregiver to our three small children at that time. But there was no satisfaction on that night, as I yearned restlessly to cover this event.

I praise God for my husband, Ricky, who is usually first to hear my countless and endless ideas, who provides wise feedback and backs me all the way. Words cannot express all that he does to help me make my dreams come true. I praise God also for my mother, Mrs. Rosetta Jamieson-Thomas, who paved the way for me through her own writing, as one of the most gifted authors of our time. I thank her for encouraging me, editing my work, and assisting me in numerous ways.

I praise God for inspiring me with the idea to write about people in my church, and I praise God for my pastor, Rev. James E. Moore, Sr., who said "Yes" when I approached him and directed me to start by interviewing the oldest members of our church family.

I praise God for the elders whose sacrifices are so easily forgotten, whose pain and prayers have ushered in the successes of the younger generation. Only God knew that their stories—their real life experiences—would provide an opportunity to chronicle American history.

I cannot thank my church family enough for trusting me with their life stories, when many of them were meeting me for the first time. Mrs. Dinah White and her grandson Mr. Duane White, Mrs. Josephine Evans and her daughter Mrs. Delores Whitehead, Mr. G. G. Woody and his wife Mrs. Beulah McClinton Woody, Mrs. Edith McIntyre and her husband Mr. Randolph McIntyre, Mrs. Merlin Bragg and her husband Mr. Theodore Bragg, Mr. Joseph Thompson and his wife Mrs. Brenda Dorsey Thompson, Mrs. Marguerite White and her family, Mrs. Marian Williams and Mrs. Barbara Turner. Many welcomed me into their homes and allowed me to probe deeply into their lives. Praise God for their vivid memories and the candid photographs they shared. I thank them for the victorious lives that they have lived and the legacy that they now give to me and all who shall read their stories. I also thank them that their legacy will extend to future generations through the proceeds that this book will raise for Second Baptist Church. May God bless each of them in Jesus' precious name!

I thank God for how all the pieces of life's puzzle fit together as my church sister Ms. Jennifer Jones won tickets to the inauguration, attended the event with other young adult church members, and shared the pictures and vivid details from her journal entry as part of the "Election Reflections" series. May God grant her success as she completes her Ph.D. and become Dr. Jennifer Jones, psychologist.

I praise God for the children He has given to my husband and me, beginning with my stepson Christopher Carty who has sought higher education at a historically black college and recently attained a 4.0 semester average. He has set a great example for his much younger siblings. Our oldest daughter Annie was one of three children under age ten, who wrote an entry for the "Election Reflections" series. This is Annie's second publication, as her work also appears in the first book published by Second Baptist Church's Christian Writers Ministry, entitled *Green Pastures*. I'm equally proud of our son Naftali and daughter Christina who were too young to participate in the project and our newest family member Baby Kayden.

In response to an open invitation for children to write letters to President Obama, Jaida and Jared Baptist rose to the challenge and submitted their wonderful entries to the "Election Reflections" series. I thank their mother Ms. Michelle Thorne for allowing them to participate, and their big sister Alaina for helping them complete the project. *I praise God for each of you. May you trust in the Lord with all your heart and acknowledge Him in all your ways, so that He shall direct you path.*

I praise God for our church secretary, Mrs. Merlin Bragg, who copied the weekly inserts for the church bulletin, and for the ushers who distributed them. Thanks to Mrs. Ruth Skerritt Abraham, Ms. Glenda Bramble, and Mrs. Louise Swinton for their counsel and encouragement.

I praise God for Reverend James Moore, Jr., who expanded our readership beyond the congregation and into cyberspace by placing the stories on the church's website where they can be accessed by readers around the world. Thanks to Sister Kareen Nazaire for assisting him in this endeavor.

I praise God for my friend Mrs. Shira Vickar Fox who suggested that I contact *The New York Times* with the story idea, and I thank reporter Mr. Kevin Coyne and photographer Mr. Timothy Ivy for covering the story.

Many prayers have been said, and I praise God that *the prayers of the righteous availeth much.*

There are always so many people behind the scenes praying and participating that I hope I acknowledged everyone. Thank you for helping me to complete my first non-fiction book. Praise the Lord! Hallelujah! Thank you, Jesus!

Sincerely,
Shauna Jamieson Carty

The "Election Reflections" series is featured in *The New York Times*

Rev. James E. Moore, Sr. (left), the pastor of Second Baptist Church, was interviewed by Mr. Kevin Coyne (right), a reporter for *The New York Times*. The interview with Mr. Coyne and some of the senior citizens took place inside the church. Mr. Timothy Ivy, a photographer for *The New York Times* and Mrs. Shauna Jamieson Carty took pictures. The story appeared in the newspaper on Sunday, January 18, 2009—two days before the inauguration of President Barack Obama; one day before the Rev. Dr. Martin Luther King Jr. holiday. "At Defining Moment, Stories of Injustice," by Kevin Coyne, generated discussion on the Internet, and some feedback including a request for a book capturing the "Election Reflections" series was sent to the church.

"Each story just brought me to tears," said Rev. Moore, Sr., who had not heard the stories prior to reading them in the "Election Reflections" series. "It's given us a very deep appreciation of what our progenitors have gone through."

The church members pictured above participated in the *New York Times* interview. From left to right, standing, are Mrs. Shauna Jamieson Carty, Mrs. Edith McIntyre, Mrs. Merlin Bragg, and Rev. James E. Moore, Sr. From left to right, seated, are Mrs. Dinah White and Mrs. Josephine Evans.

Mr. Timothy Ivy, a photographer for *The New York Times,* photographs Mrs. Josephine Evans, as Mrs. Edith McIntyre looks on. Mrs. Evans was accompanied by her daughter Mrs. Delores Whitehead who also participated in the interview.

Second Baptist Church occupies a corner lot at 200 Locust Street and Second
Avenue in Roselle, New Jersey. The church celebrated its 118th anniversary in 2008.
Since then, renovations have been made by adding a wheelchair ramp and other
accommodations to improve access for elderly and disabled congregants.

Mrs. Dinah White and her grandson Mr. Duane White pose in front of a family portrait in her home as they share their thoughts on the election of President Barack Obama. Mr. White took his grandmother to vote and kept her abreast of the results as they were reported on television on Election Night 2008. Mrs. White persistently prayed for President Obama's safety.

Nation's first black president overcomes a legacy of hate

Mrs. Dinah White tells her story:

Mrs. Dinah White was younger than seven years old when she watched a group of white men murder her teenage uncle by placing a noose around his neck and hanging him from a tree. The incident devastated her family and made a permanent impression on her of race relations at its worst in the United States. The election of the first African American president of this country was something Mrs. White thought she would never live to see. Senator Barack Obama won the election one month after Mrs. White's eighty-eighth birthday. She believes that the election of an African American president shows more racial harmony, but we still have a long way to go.

Election Day 2008:

Mrs. White traveled to Abraham Clark High School to cast her vote. Mr. Duane White, her forty-five year old grandson, drove her there from their home in Roselle. They had been focused on the news all morning and had heard about how long the lines were. Mr. White wanted to be sure his grandmother wouldn't grow weary while waiting, so he brought a folding chair, but she didn't use it because at mid-day, the lines were fairly short.

Fear for his life:

That night, Mrs. White stayed up late awaiting the results. She felt nervous for Senator Obama and his family, just as she had been during his campaign. Her experiences with racism had taught her a tough lesson about hate, and she feared for Senator Obama's life.

"I was quite upset because I just knew that even before he won the election, somebody was gonna kill him," she said.

While she was listening to the news, her grandson would run downstairs periodically to make sure she was keeping up with the results. She paid close attention to the states she used to live in, or was familiar with from her childhood. These were states where she had heard terrible stories of racism and discrimination. "I was surprised that McCain didn't win Virginia," she said. "I was surprised at North Carolina."

Senator Obama's opponent, Senator John McCain, won in South Carolina, and Mrs. White was not surprised that a white male had won there. Mrs. White was born in South Carolina, and as a child, she had witnessed the tragic lynching of her uncle in front of her grandparents' home.

Lynch* mob murders a teenage boy:

"I keep getting flashbacks," Mrs. White explained. "I'll never forget. Sometimes, I can see it. They lynched my uncle in the yard." A pained expression contorted her face as she described what happened to her uncle, Charlie James, who was a teenage boy when he was murdered. "He came running and telling my grandmother and grandfather. He said he didn't get off the white lady's path fast enough." Her uncle outran the men who followed him home. When they arrived, they told everybody to get out the house, but Mrs. White's grandmother moved quickly and hid the children in the cellar, a hole in the ground that had been dug at the side of the house. Mrs. White cowered there in fear, holding the baby. Big Momma (her grandmother) had told her to keep the baby quiet by shoving a sock in the baby's mouth. The children peeked out to see what was happening to their family from their hiding place.

"They made them watch. They didn't know we were around… What they did to my uncle was terrible… They left him hanging from a tree."

New president signals a brighter future:

More than eighty years later, the memory of that tragic day is still vivid in Mrs. White's mind. She feels grateful that although she experienced many other incidents of racism and discrimination in her lifetime, she also noticed positive changes. Her children and grandchildren who were born in New Jersey have had better opportunities than she had when she was growing up. She views the election of America's first black president as a sign that her great-grandchildren will face even greater opportunities.

She offers this advice for incoming President Barack Obama: "Ask God to guide him. Believe in yourself. Some people believe in everyone but themselves."

-Reported by Shauna Jamieson Carty

Historical Note

President-elect Barack Obama, his wife future First Lady Michelle, and their daughters Sasha and Malia are said to have the style and beauty of the late President John F. Kennedy and his family.

When President-elect Obama speaks, he captivates and inspires his audience with a message of hope that is reminiscent of the messages of hope delivered by the late Rev. Dr. Martin Luther King.

Senator Robert Kennedy was assassinated in 1968 and Rev. Dr. King was also murdered during that same year. People who are familiar with these tragic events fear for President-elect Barack Obama's life.

- **Prayer Point:** *We pray that God would protect President Barack Obama, his wife Michelle, and their daughters Sasha and Malia, in Jesus' name. Amen.*

*Definitions:** The American Heritage Dictionary defines ***lynch*** as to execute, especially to hang, without due process of the law. During the period when Mrs. White's uncle was lynched, whites in some parts of the South used lynching to strike fear in the hearts of blacks and keep them in their place. The NAACP and the Tuskegee Institute maintain statistics on lynching in American history.

Mrs. Josephine Taylor Evans and her daughter Mrs. Delores Whitehead prayed for President Barack Obama and rejoiced in his victory on Election Day. Looking forward to Inauguration Day, they posed with a picture of the new First Family: the president, his wife First Lady Michelle Obama, and their daughters Sasha and Malia.

First black president overcomes one hurdle; African Americans face another

Mrs. Josephine Evans tells her story:

Mrs. Josephine Taylor Evans was a college student when she got her first full-time job earning four dollars a week. A white family employed her to live with them to do the cooking, cleaning, and taking care of their small child, she said. Today, her great-granddaughter attends college, earns twice as much in just an hour, and faces fewer restrictions because of her race. Their family watched the election, thankful that Americans have overcome racism enough to elect their first black president. Yet, Mrs. Evans' family bears a personal loss that is becoming too familiar to American black families.

"As Christians, we have to keep the faith and run this race for a very long time," Mrs. Evans wrote in a note about the election. "We have also been singing this song for many years, 'We shall overcome some day'… Well that day has arrived! Praise the Lord."

An American Family Moves Forward

A look at Mrs. Evans' family history illustrates a story of progress throughout the generations. She was born in a one-room log cabin in North Carolina in 1916. Her family farmed their own food and sewed her dresses. As a child, she attended a one-room school where children of all ages were taught. Her father labored, chopping wood to scrape together the savings to send her to Fayetteville State College to become a teacher. Financial struggles caused her to leave college after two years and return to the farm to help her parents with sharecropping and caring for her younger siblings.

Decades later, Mrs. Evans' daughter, Mrs. Delores Whitehead, finished college and went on to earn a Master's degree. She served as a librarian at the Newark Public Library until her recent retirement.

Today, Mrs. Evans' great-granddaughter Jaide Lee is preparing to graduate with a four-year college degree after only three years. She saved herself a year by taking college courses while she was still in high school. As a member of the National Honor Society, she has been invited to attend incoming President Obama's inauguration. Her sister Tyra Lee turned eighteen in time to vote for the first time in this election. She is a high school senior and plans to attend college next year.

Youth Violence Claims Lives

As the years pass, and opportunities increase for African Americans, not all African Americans are allowed to live out their dreams. Yet, it is black on black crime, and not racism that often steals their life.

Youth violence leaves families grieving, with great concern about how violence is claiming the lives of so many sons and daughters in the black community. Violence left two mothers from Second Baptist Church grieving the loss of their sons. Two other sons miraculously survived multiple gunshot wounds. While the tragic incidents were unrelated, they stemmed from youth violence.

Some black youth are excelling and using their education to blaze a trail of success, but others are abandoning their education and succumbing to the ills of drugs and gangs. Youth violence devastates families and destroys communities.

Election Results Inspire Hope

Mrs. Evans prays that the election of America's first black president will inspire young people to study hard and use education to better themselves and improve their communities.

"I truly hope that everyone will work for peace and love and understanding and try to make this world a better place where we all are trying to live."

A Note from the White House

On Mrs. Evans' 95th birthday, in 2011, she received a greeting signed by President Obama and the First Lady which reads, *"We are pleased to join your family and friends in wishing you the best on your birthday. Your generation has shown the courage to persevere through moments of uncertainty and challenge, and your story is an important part of the American narrative. We hope you look back with joy and pride on the many contributions and memories made over the course of your life.*

We wish you health and happiness in the years ahead."

-Reported by Shauna Jamieson Carty

Historical Note

The successful election of the first black president of the United States attains a new level of equality for blacks—one that many people thought they would never live to see. There is a brief, yet detailed, explanation of how black Americans were denied equality throughout American history on jfklibrary.org, the library dedicated to President John F. Kennedy.

President John F. Kennedy was assassinated on November 22, 1963. To read more about President Kennedy's involvement in the Civil Rights Movement to attain equality for black Americans, visit jfklibrary.org. His brother, **Senator Robert Kennedy**, another champion for equal rights for blacks, was assassinated in 1968. He managed the campaign that secured his brother's win to become President in 1960. Senator Kennedy was campaigning to become the Democratic Candidate for the presidency. To read more about Senator Kennedy, visit arlingtoncemetary.org.

- **Prayer Point:** *We pray that God would guide our nation and protect President Barack Obama, his wife First Lady Michelle, their daughters Sasha and Malia, and their grandmother, in Jesus' name. Amen.*

Roselle businessman Mr. G. G. Woody and his wife Mrs. Beulah McClinton Woody operate G.G. Woody Funeral Home in Roselle, New Jersey. Together, they awaited the election results at home.

Mr. G. G. Woody and his daughter Leslie Woody, who is his partner in the funeral home, posed in front of a wall of historical memorabilia including an invitation from President John F. Kennedy. President Barack Obama's election brought back memories for Mr. G. G. Woody who was the first black councilman elected in Roselle, New Jersey.

The road to the White House:
Roselle's first black Councilman
helps to pave the way

Roselle Businessman G. G. Woody tells his story:

During the campaign leading up to the presidential election, Mr. G.G. Woody had an answer for everyone he met who said they feared that if a black man won, he would be assassinated. He told them to vote for Senator Barack Obama anyway.

"We gotta do it," he told them. "This is our great chance."

On election night, Mr. Woody watched the election results with his wife, Mrs. Beulah McClinton Woody. From the comfort of their home in Roselle, they wondered if Americans had changed enough to elect the first African American president. History had also taught them that if Senator Obama won, there was a possibility that someone would try to kill him.

"People are still afraid of losing him that way," Mr. Woody said. He explained that the fear stems from the 1960s when three men who advocated equal rights for African Americans were assassinated. "It's a horrible feeling. They understand how they felt when Martin was killed, how they felt when President Kennedy was killed, how they felt when Bobby was killed; all the people who sacrificed their lives to voter registration in the South."

Most Americans have only seen Rev. Dr. Martin Luther King, Jr., former President Kennedy and Senator Robert "Bobby" Kennedy on television, or read about them in history books. Mr. Woody knew some of them personally. During the 1950s, Mr. Woody became the first black councilman elected in Roselle.

"There were only a handful of black elected officials in the country and we all knew one another," Mr. Woody said.

His prominence as one of few black politicians at that time led him to meeting other people who were involved in the struggle to overcome discrimination and obtain equal opportunities for African Americans. He possesses pictures and documents that capture significant moments from that era. An invitation to the White House is mounted in a frame on one wall of his house. A picture of Mr. Woody standing beside Senator Robert Kennedy hangs nearby. Another photograph shows Mr. Woody standing with the son of Rev. Dr. Martin Luther King, Jr.

Mr. Woody was among the elected officials who paved the way for the election of America's first black president. He explained that he recognizes that people's attitudes have changed.

"That tells me that younger people are thinking differently," Mr. Woody said, citing the number of white Americans who voted for President-elect Obama. "The younger people are getting to know one another to respect one another."

Mr. Woody feels optimistic about the future and praises God for the progress people have made. "He's working His way in His own time because somehow Obama came and Obama is from a mixed heritage. That in turn is bringing respect from all around the world. He has to be God sent."

-Reported by Shauna Jamieson Carty

Historical Note

This photograph of Mr. G.G. Woody (farthest right) and Senator Robert Kennedy hangs on the wall of Mr. Woody's home in Roselle among other historical memorabilia. Mr. Woody was the first black person elected as a councilman in Roselle, and one of the first three African Americans to serve as an elected official in the state of New Jersey.

Prayer Point: We *pray for peace, in Jesus' name. Amen.*

Mrs. Edith McIntyre and her husband Mr. Randolph McIntyre, Sr. raised their son Randolph, Jr., "Randy" in Roselle, New Jersey, where he had more opportunities than they had growing up in the South, restricted by segregation.

Faith, fearlessness, and focus forecast a brighter future

Mrs. Edith McIntyre tells her story:

From her childhood in a segregated town in North Carolina, to her career in New York City, Mrs. Edith McIntyre strived to shake off society's restrictions. She strikes a balance between appreciating where she came from and embracing where she is going. Her experience has great personal value, and it is also symbolic of the history of the United States, before and after the election of the first African American president.

""I agree with the statement that we can have the knowledge without letting it have us,'" said Mrs. McIntyre, who celebrated her seventy-second birthday in March. The home she shares with her husband Mr. Randolph McIntyre, Sr., is a great distance from the poor housing in North Carolina where she was born.

She remembers that she, along with her sister and five brothers, faced trials and lacked some material things, but their courageous mother enriched their lives.

"She was diminutive in size, but she was so brave and humble. She was great!" Mrs. McIntyre said, describing her mother. Mary Ann McNeil Walker wanted more for her children than the life that she had as a laundry presser. She gave Mrs. McIntyre and her siblings this advice: "Do the best you can. Don't look to the right or the left; just keep focus." And although they lived in a segregated town, Mrs. Walker developed a friendship with a white lady for whom she did laundry. She also took her children to sing in a white school and a white church.

As a result, Mrs. McIntyre and her siblings felt confident and secure, even though the law restricted them to riding in the back of the bus, using colored water fountains, and standing to eat meals at food counters where whites were allowed to sit.

"We did not develop any fear or inferior feeling toward those of other races," said Mrs. McIntyre. "I didn't have any fear of other races because of the way I was raised."

Her mother also taught them to put their faith in God, and Mrs. McIntyre said that Philippians 3:13-14 has helped her navigate the changes in her life. It reads, "Brethren, I do not count myself to have apprehended; but one thing I do, forgetting those things which are behind and reaching forward to those things which are ahead, I press toward the goal for the prize of the upward calling of God in Christ Jesus."

She completed high school at age seventeen and had no money to attend college. Through work-study, God made a way for her to obtain a Bachelor of Science degree at Fayetteville State Teacher's College. As she pressed on, she worked and was able to pay for her studies. She attained a Master of Arts degree in Curriculum and Teaching from Columbia University. Years later, while she and her husband were living in New Jersey and she was working in New York, God provided a scholarship for her to earn a Master's degree in Social Work from Rutgers University.

In many situations, she found herself to be a racial minority, yet her mother's teaching and her faith in God helped her to excel. She also had the support of a loving husband and her extended family who took care of her son, Randolph "Randy" McIntyre, Jr. while she studied. Her family remains close knit today.

Mrs. McIntyre credits another person with being "an angel of mercy" who was important to her biological, social, and spiritual development. "She was my paternal aunt Mrs. Zilphia Mae Walker Towns, (Aunt Zif), a surrogate mother for one of my brothers and me. She was caring, compassionate, and generous and sought no glory for her charitable efforts. Her giving delivered gifts to move one forward, not bribes to shackle one to her expectations." President Barack Obama also benefited from the loving care of two women: his mother and maternal grandmother.

On the night of the election, Mrs. McIntyre watched the election results at home with her husband. "I just kept hoping so strongly and saying a little prayer: Let him win. And when he did, it happened so fast, it was joyfully mind boggling."

President-elect Barack Obama's victory sparked another personal celebration for Mrs. McIntyre, like the one she felt when the American government outlawed segregation and she no longer had to ride in the back of the bus.

"Someone has said, we should head toward a color blind nation," said Mrs. McIntyre. "We want to get to the place where we support each other equally… Should the trend continue, it can only get better."

-Reported by Shauna Jamieson Carty

Historical Note

Power of a praying grandparent

On the day I interviewed Mrs. Edith McIntyre, she awoke at 2 a.m. to pray. She remained in prayer, meditation, and Bible reading for about four hours that morning. While this practice of praying long before the Lord may not be unique to black grandparents, it seems that this continual prayer sustained our ancestors, and helped them overcome slavery, segregation, and other acts of discrimination.

As a child, I shared a bedroom with my grandmother. I remember asking her why she prayed so long. She prayed about everything and for everyone. Another senior citizen whom I've adopted as an uncle habitually rose at 3 a.m. to pray through until daylight. Another grandmother, who is a mother of six grown children, rises at 3 a.m. to read her Bible and pray. For many of these prayer warriors, praying and Bible reading go hand in hand. On November 21, 2008, Pastor James Moore, Sr. led Second Baptist Church in an all night prayer session, from midnight to 6 a.m. Many of the congregants who endured through the night were senior citizens.

Prayer point: "Father God, I pray for our president that he loves and practices mercy and justice, praises and adores God (verse 1*); acts wisely, lives a life of integrity both in public and in private, senses and knows the presence of God in his life (2); hates evil, will not tolerate compromise in his life or in those who surround him (3); keeps his heart right with God and man, repents of sin and fights against it (4); hates and avoids pride, evil talk, and slander (5); appoints blameless and efficient men and women to positions of authority (6); maintains blameless and godly standard (7); labors with all strength to eradicate wrongdoing, immoral laws, and to build a righteous foundation for the nation (8); I pray that lies and deceit are unacceptable to him (7)--in Jesus' name. Amen." (*Psalm 101)

Mrs. Edith McIntyre uses Psalm 101 to guide her in praying for President-elect Barack Obama. She obtained this prayer guide from a booklet that was compiled by former Second Baptist Church member Carlene Pierce. The original Psalm 101 guide to Praying for the President was created by Dr. Kevin Meador for Prayer Closet Ministries, Inc., and it is available on their web site for use in intercessory prayer.

Mr. and Mrs. Bragg attended an integrated high school in New Jersey during the 1940s, but after graduating from high school, Mr. Bragg went down South to prepare to serve his country in the military. It was then that he learned how separate and unequal living conditions were for black people. That experience influenced his decision to vote for President Barack Obama.

Presidential Election 2008
Something to *Bragg* about...

Mr. and Mrs. Bragg tell their story:

For the first time during their fifty-seven years of marriage, Mr. Theodore Bragg and his wife Mother Merlin Bragg disagreed about which candidate to vote for in the presidential election. During the Democratic primary, Mrs. Bragg supported Senator Hillary Clinton. Mr. Bragg felt that then-Senator Barack Obama deserved the chance to represent the Democratic Party.

"I changed her mind. I stayed on her back," said Mr. Bragg.

"He said, 'You've got to vote for him. You've got to give him a shot,'" his wife confirmed.

Her support for Senator Clinton wavered as she learned more about President-elect Obama's background and all that he and his wife had accomplished. This led her to agree with her husband, whom she had known since elementary school.

The Braggs shared a similar background, growing up in New Jersey during the 1930s and 1940s. They have similar memories of life in the North. They both attended school in Roselle, where blacks and whites learned alongside each other in the classroom.

"We had integration here as far as we can remember, but there were some social differences," said Mrs. Bragg.

They remember that the school buses were reserved for Jewish students who were bused pass Lincoln School and Harrison School to Chestnut Street School. As children, the Braggs walked to school, but they remember that there were some white children who walked too.

Mrs. Bragg moved to Linden at age 12, and found that she had even fewer black classmates and neighbors than she had in Roselle.

"We were the first African Americans on the street," said Mrs. Bragg. "We all got along well. We did not realize the prejudice that was in the South."

After their high school graduation, Mr. Bragg joined the military and was sent down South to Georgia for training.

"That's when I hit segregation," said Mr. Bragg. Almost 20 years old, and eager to fight for his country, Mr. Bragg now had to learn that he needed to step aside if he saw a white person coming down the street. Dressed in full uniform, he now had to ride in the back of the bus. He had to go hungry once while traveling from the South to visit his wife in New Jersey because a train station attendant in Washington, DC, refused to serve him a hot dog.

"There was no reacting to it," said Mr. Bragg. "You just did what you know you were supposed to do. You didn't fight anything because you didn't have any win."

On the surface, Mr. Bragg said the experiences didn't bother him, but on that visit, he vented his frustration and humiliation to his wife when he got home. The discrimination continued overseas.

"I saw a change in France," said Mr. Bragg. "When I first got there, the company was segregated. In July 1952, they took half the company and sent to another company." He remembers the white soldiers as being upset over this forced integration.

Mrs. Bragg remained in New Jersey and enjoyed friendly relations with the whites for whom she worked. She passed a Civil Service exam and landed her first job.

"I became the typist to eleven men and they were all white," said Mrs. Bragg. "The eleven white men treated me like a queen."

After the birth of the Bragg's third child, Mrs. Bragg became a stay-at-home mom for the next 17 years. Her husband returned to New Jersey right before their first child was born and found work in less than a week. In 1956, he returned to work in Abraham Clark High School, eight years after his graduation from there.

While American society has undergone tremendous change around them, Mr. Bragg's love for the woman he's known since childhood remains deep. They're pleased with the love that they see President-elect Obama showing for his wife future First Lady Michelle.

-Reported by Shauna Jamieson Carty

Historical Note

While segregation prevailed in the South, Mr. and Mrs. Bragg grew up attending integrated schools in New Jersey, as depicted in their high school yearbook photographs. Abraham Clark High School yearbook "The Clarker" 1948 shows Mr. Bragg (left column, second row).

Prayer Point: Our Father, we thank you for the example of love and commitment we see in President-elect Obama and his wife, and in the Braggs. We pray that you continue to bind them together in love with cords that cannot be broken. Please bless and protect the men and women you have joined together, Lord—in Jesus' name. Amen.

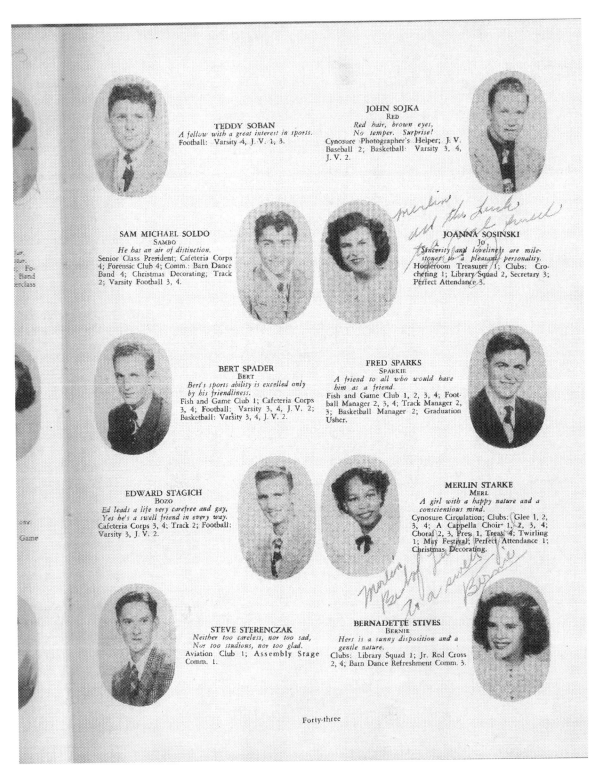

TEDDY SOBAN
A fellow with a great interest in sports.
Football: Varsity 4, J. V. 1, 3.

JOHN SOJKA
RED
Red hair, brown eyes,
No temper. Surprise!
Cynosure Photographer's Helper; J. V.
Baseball 2; Basketball: Varsity 3, 4,
J. V. 2.

SAM MICHAEL SOLDO
SAMBO
He has an air of distinction.
Senior Class President; Cafeteria Corps
4; Forensic Club 4; Comm.: Barn Dance
Band 4; Christmas Decorating; Track
2; Varsity Football 3, 4.

JOANNA SOSINSKI
JO
Sincerity and loveliness are mile-
stones to a pleasant personality.
Homeroom Treasurer 1; Clubs: Cro-
cheting 1; Library Squad 2, Secretary 3;
Perfect Attendance 3.

BERT SPADER
BERT
Bert's sports ability is excelled only
by his friendliness.
Fish and Game Club 1; Cafeteria Corps
3, 4; Football: Varsity 3, 4, J. V. 2;
Basketball: Varsity 3, 4, J. V. 2.

FRED SPARKS
SPARKIE
A friend to all who would have
him as a friend.
Fish and Game Club 1, 2, 3, 4; Foot-
ball Manager 2, 3, 4; Track Manager 2,
3; Basketball Manager 2; Graduation
Usher.

EDWARD STAGICH
BOZO
Ed leads a life very carefree and gay,
Yet he's a swell friend in every way.
Cafeteria Corps 3, 4; Track 2; Football:
Varsity 3, J. V. 2.

MERLIN STARKE
MERL
A girl with a happy nature and a
conscientious mind.
Cynosure Circulation; Clubs: Glee 1, 2,
3, 4; A Cappella Choir 1, 2, 3, 4;
Choral 2, 3, Pres. 1, Treas. 4; Twirling
1; May Festival; Perfect Attendance 1;
Christmas Decorating.

STEVE STERENCZAK
Neither too careless, nor too sad,
Nor too studious, nor too glad.
Aviation Club 1; Assembly Stage
Comm. 1.

BERNADETTE STIVES
BERNIE
Hers is a sunny disposition and a
gentle nature.
Clubs: Library Squad 1; Jr. Red Cross
2, 4; Barn Dance Refreshment Comm. 3.

Forty-three

Linden High School yearbook "Cynosure" 1949 shows Mrs. Bragg (right column, fourth row)

Mr. Joe Thompson and his wife Mrs. Brenda Dorsey Thompson marched on Washington during the Civil Rights movement. Today, they can be spotted worshipping the Lord at Second Baptist Church.

Election victory raises the perception of a black man's worth

Mr. Joseph Thompson tells his story:

At the end of the day, Mr. Joseph Thompson (Brother Joe) is a husband who loves and appreciates his wife, a father whose concern for his children and grandchildren knows no end, and a Christian filled with hope, joy, and faith in God. Yet, while he was growing up, there were times when his life experience caused him to question his own worth. Like the time when his three cousins were killed by white men and there was nothing Brother Joe and his family could do about it. It was hard for him to imagine then, that a little black boy would grow up to win the presidential election in 2008.

"Today, I'm flabbergasted that the President of the United States is a black man," said Brother Joe. "If I was 15 years old and somebody told me, it would be too far-fetched."

Brother Joe was born in Georgetown, South Carolina in 1938, and grew up at a time when a white person could take a black person's life and there was nothing the grieving family could do about it.

"As I was growing up, I don't remember any white person living there. But they would visit to invoke fear," Brother Joe said. "I've had a cross burned in the yard of the house I grew up in."

His father and uncle owned 65 acres of woodland and they would sell timber to the International Paper Company. They engaged in business, but they didn't have the right to vote, nor could they use the justice system for their family's protection.

A common pastime for boys was to go to the woods where they would hunt with rifles they got from their family. Brother Joe used to go to the woods with his cousins, but he'll never forget one time when he stayed home. On that day, his three cousins never returned. Their family found their bodies punctured with gunshot wounds and tied up to a tree. They believe that his cousins were killed by a group of white men who were drunk and out hunting.

These experiences left Brother Joe feeling that there was nothing equal about whites and blacks. They didn't have equal rights and opportunities, and they were not treated equally by the law.

"In your mind, you said this is never going to change," said Brother Joe.

As a young adult, he got involved in trying to bring about change. He went to live in Newark in 1958, where he met Brenda Dorsey who would later become his wife.

"When I came here, they were organizing the March on Washington, D.C.," said Brother Joe. He and his wife joined the men and women who marched on Washington on more than one occasion. He grew a beard and an afro as a sign of protest, and briefly became a Black Panther.

"You were such a standout when you became a Black Panther that your life became vulnerable," Brother Joe said, explaining why he didn't remain a member of that group for long.

Brother Joe and his wife had four children: Joseph, Jr., "Jay," Traci, April, and Gabril. He went with his older son Jay to vote at Borough Hall in Roselle on Election Day.

"I vote. That's something that was very vital to me because I remember when I couldn't," said Brother Joe. "My father couldn't. My mother couldn't. I wish they could be alive today to see this new president. It would be like a gift."

Brother Joe feels optimistic about the future, and the impact that the first African American President will make. "It's gonna get better for blacks in this country. It's gonna lift black people's mind about where they are and what they have accomplished."

Life has taken Brother Joe on one adventure after another. His greatest joy is not political; it's personal. He recently became a born again Christian. "When it happened for me, I couldn't stop enjoying it. I couldn't believe the joy. It was a whole beautiful thing."

-Reported by Shauna Jamieson Carty

Historical Note

The following excerpt is quoted verbatim from the John F. Kennedy Presidential Library, JFK in history: Civil Rights Context in the Early 1960s

"Slavery and the Founding of the Nation: The Three-Fifths Compromise

When our nation was founded, despite the stirring claim that "all men are created equal," enslaved blacks were not fully regarded as men and women, but were thought of instead as the legal property of their owners. At the Constitutional Convention in 1787, fifteen of the fifty-five delegates who convened in Philadelphia to write a new Constitution for the American republic were slave owners. Slavery became a major issue when the delegates considered the apportioning of seats for the House of Representatives – which was calculated as one seat for every 30,000 inhabitants. Southern delegates insisted on full representation based on the free and slave populations of the South. Northern delegates argued that slaves were regarded as property not as citizens and, therefore, should not be counted toward apportioning seats in Congress. The issue threatened to break up the Convention until the 3/5 compromise was adopted: 50,000 slaves would be regarded as equivalent to 30,000 free persons. Or, put another way, one slave was, for the purposes of representation, 3/5 of a free person."

SOURCE: http://www.jfklibrary.org/Historical+Resources/JFK+in+History/Civil+Rights+Context+in+the+Early+1960s.htm

Prayer Point: Father God, we pray for our nation, that we may truly love you with all our heart, soul, mind and strength, and love our neighbor as we love our self. Please help us to forgive each other as you have forgiven us. In Jesus' name. Amen.

This family portrait shows a younger Mrs. Marguerite White (center) flanked by her six children: Jo-Ann, Jerilyn "Jill", Janet, Jacqueline, June, and Jeffrey.

President Barack Obama:
A Source of Inspiration to American Families

Mrs. Marguerite White tells her story:

Mrs. Marguerite White plans to be fixed in front of her television this Tuesday, watching the inauguration of the first African American president of the United States—and she would love to offer him some advice.

"Don't forget God. Always put Him first. As long as we put Him first, we can make it," she said.

By putting her faith in God, Mrs. White endured the trials she has had to face. She was a child during the Great Depression, and she remembers how her family made much with the little they had.

"Everybody was so kindhearted," she said. "All the neighbors helped each other."

She remembers her parents being on welfare for some time. They would join the food line at the firehouse to get flour, bread, and cans of food. If one neighbor missed out on the food line, the other neighbors would say, "Here. Take this."

In 1946, she married Mr. James White, Jr., her lifelong friend who attended school with her and used to live across the street from her parents' house. God blessed them with five daughters and a son, but Mr. White passed away when the children were young. After he passed, Mrs. White moved back to her childhood home in Roselle, where her parents Harry and Cornelia Armstrong helped her raise her children.

Mrs. Cornelia Armstrong was a Deaconess at Second Baptist Church and remained active there until her passing in 1996. The program from her funeral service reads: "The Triumphant Homegoing Service of Deaconess Cornelia Armstrong" and reflects her reliance on God that she taught to her children and grandchildren. It reads: "Prayer was and is the sustaining force in our lives and 'faith' is the key that unlocks the door." We walk by faith, not by sight. 2 Corinthians 5:7

Mrs. White suggests that President Obama must rely on God to guide him, as he inherits and tries to correct the problems that faced the Bush Administration. People have been losing their jobs and their homes today, just as she remembers they were during the Depression. She has observed that neighbors no longer seem friendly and willing to share.

"Everything is expensive," she said. "The taxes are so high; you can barely pay them. Almost every time you get your tax bill, it gets higher and higher. I could cry."

Without the help of her daughters--the third generation of the Armstrong family to live in their home--she could not afford to remain there.

"I just pray: Lord, please help me," she said.

Mrs. White grew up attending school side by side with black and white students, playing with white friends. Yet, she said she was aware of prejudice and felt that discrimination could stop a black man from fulfilling his potential. As a result, she had not expected the historic results.

"I was very glad Obama got it," she said. "No, I didn't think it would ever happen. What a surprise! What a pleasant surprise! I was hollering with all the crowd and clapping and crying."

She prayed and trusted in the Lord Jesus as she raised her six children, and she now prays daily for President Obama: **"Lord, please help him. Please guide Him. Because we sure do need the Lord and He can fix things like nobody else can."**

-Reported by Shauna Jamieson Carty

Historical Note

An Inauguration Day Like No Other

Americans will travel from all over the country to attend the Inauguration of the first African American president of the United States—with or without an invitation. Private individuals and churches have organized bus rides into Washington, D.C. Employees plan to take the day off from work. Some parents plan to take their children out of school, so families can be together to watch the event. Many schools and offices will be closed on the day before Inauguration Day to observe Rev. Dr. Martin Luther King's birthday. The election of President Barack Obama is a fulfillment of Rev. Dr. Marin Luther King's dream.

Second Baptist Church will hold an Inauguration Brunch in the Fellowship Hall on Tuesday, January 20, 2009 beginning at 10:45 a.m. Members of our church family will bring refreshments and gather to watch the historic event together on big screen TV.

- **Prayer Point:** We pray that God would guide our nation and protect President Barack Obama, his wife First Lady Michelle, their daughters Sasha and Malia, and their grandmother, in Jesus' name. Amen.

Mrs. Marian Williams (left) and her sister Mrs. Barbara Turner are pleased to note how attentive President Obama is to his family. The president reminds them of their own father who raised nine children, first with his wife, and then alone for many years after she passed away. He was his daughters' role model.

A good father is no stranger to black families

Two sisters, Mrs. Marian Briggs Williams and Mrs. Barbara Briggs Turner, tell their story.

As the image of President Barack Obama with his wife First Lady Michelle, and their two daughters Sasha and Malia flashes across the television screen into homes around the world, it shatters stereotypes because the American media more commonly portrays criminalized black men. Like many black husbands and fathers before him, President Obama is an outstanding role model.

Mrs. Marian Briggs Williams was born in 1930 and grew up with a strong black father. Mr. Alexander Briggs married Lillian Edmonds Briggs. They moved north from Petersburg, Virginia in 1925, after the birth of their second child. They lived in Cranford and Roselle Park before settling in Roselle, where Mr. Briggs established Briggs Sign Shop and became nationally renowned for his slogan, "Who knows without A sign." A newspaper article from the "Afro Magazine Section" of a newspaper dated December 7, 1957 states that Mr. Briggs was "the first colored person to serve on a jury in the Fifth Judicial District Court in 1941..." He was also a Trustee at Second Baptist Church in Roselle.

Sadly, Mr. Briggs lost his wife and mother of their nine children in 1943. At that time, Mrs. William's youngest sibling, Mrs. Barbara Turner, was only seven; their oldest sibling was 23.

"When I was working at AT&T and we had classes, the instructor asked us to point out who was a good example of a role model," said Mrs. Williams. "Most mentioned celebrities. When they asked me, I said my father. My mother died when I was 13 and he raised us. We all had good jobs and good reputations and honesty."

As Mrs. Williams learned about President Obama during the campaign, she was impressed by him, and was not surprised that he won the election. She described how she responded to someone who was less optimistic: "Someone said, we're never going to have a black president. They're not going to have a black man in the White House. I thought, eventually we will. Things have been changing all along. Eventually, it had to come to pass." To her, it seemed to take a long time, considering that Rev. Dr. Martin Luther King, Jr. rose to leadership during the 1960s and it's taken over 40 years for another black leader to earn the support of all races throughout the nation.

At age 78, Mrs. Williams is vibrant, energetic and physically fit. "I'm blessed," she says, giving God total praise for her well being. She and her sister Mrs. Turner are the only two of the nine siblings remaining. They both grew up in Roselle and attended schools here as members of a black minority in a predominantly white school system.

"When we were growing up, we were raised to know people for the content of their character, not the color of their skin," Mrs. Turner said. "I appreciate that because you get to know everyone, different nationalities and backgrounds. That was among the standards our father set for us."

Consequently, they enjoyed school and had a diverse group of friends. Yet they were not immune to racial prejudice and they were aware that some people applied different standards to people of different races. Their family broke through many barriers to become the first black person in various positions. Their late sister Mrs. Louise Briggs West was the first woman sprayer at the General Motors plant. Mrs. Williams was the first black salesperson at a store in Newark. And their father was the only black person employed by another business in Roselle, while he maintained his sign shop.

"He was lettering the trucks and equipment there," Mrs. Williams said. "They were having a formal Christmas party and dad bought mother a new gown The men that were working there were all white and didn't want my parents to attend, so they didn't go. They didn't end up going. When my mother died a couple years later, she got buried in that gown."

Mrs. Turner acknowledges that the nation has made great strides toward racial harmony, but there is still work to be done. "You still have prejudice to this day," she said.

The satisfaction of seeing President Barack Obama take the oath of office to become President last Tuesday eclipsed the memories of past discrimination and present-day imperfection.

"I was really overjoyed," said Mrs. Turner, who turned 72 on Inauguration Day. "What an awesome birthday gift!" "God had predestined him to be where he is now."

Mrs. Williams and her daughter Ms. Sharon Smith, along with Mrs. Turner and her daughter Rev. Barbara Turner, watched the Inauguration at a celebratory brunch at Second Baptist Church.

"It was great," said Mrs. Williams, who remains active in the NAACP and the National Council Negro Women. Her advice for young people: "Take advantage of the opportunities that you have now, get a good education, set goals for yourself, believe things will get better, have faith in God and pray."

-Reported by Shauna Jamieson Carty

Historical Note

Second Baptist Church celebrated Inauguration Day with a brunch. Members watched the events of the day on big screen television. They also watched the movie *Selma Lord Selma* to reflect on how far the nation has come.

Prayer Point: May God continue to bless, guide, and protect President Barack Obama and his family, in Jesus' name.

· ·

A newspaper clipping shows Mr. Alexander Briggs, who established Briggs Sign Shop in Roselle and became nationally renowned for his slogan, "Who knows without a sign." Mr. Briggs was Mrs. Marian Williams' father and role model.

Ms. Jennifer Jones won tickets to the inauguration of President Obama.
She attended with her friend Ms. Wendy Adi-Darko and captured
the experience on camera and through her journal entry.

Second Baptist Church Members Attend the Inauguration

-from the diary of Ms. Jennifer Jones

1/16/09: My friend Wendy and I both took off Monday, Tuesday, and Wednesday of next week to head to Washington for the inauguration. We booked the hotel back in October even before Barack Obama won the election. We both knew he was going to win! We also put our names on the list for tickets to the inauguration. Today, Rene from Sen. Menendez' office called. Out of 30,000 people who put their names on the list, I have 2 of the 347 tickets. I have butterflies in my stomach just thinking about not only being in DC but being at the base of the Capitol steps watching Barack Obama become our 44th president…

1/17/09: Wendy and I got on the road at about 6:00pm. Neither of us could contain our excitement. We were on our way to Washington (well, Baltimore for today) but you know what I mean! We sang and laughed the whole ride. We passed so many buses along the way. I couldn't help but to wonder… "Is that one headed to Washington?" We pulled up to the Hilton in Baltimore and there was a charter bus filled with people. The lobby was packed with teenagers checking in. The energy in the lobby (even though we were still 25 miles from Washington) was amazing… We had CNN on earlier and we were watching Barack Obama's train ride from Philly to Washington. Obama was standing in the crowds shaking hands and taking pictures. I felt like Barack is one of us… he's not unreachable… he's not untouchable… but he truly is one of us. But to be honest a part of me was scared that he was too out in the open. There's this fear that something might happen before Tuesday, but then I remembered God has not given us the Spirit of fear. So again, I can't wait to see Barack Obama standing on those steps and taking that precious oath to become our 44th president. Wow those words feel so powerful and I am so proud that I am able to write them.

1/18/09: Everyone is telling me to write how I feel about this extraordinary event... well, how do I feel? I can remember being 8 years old, sitting in my third grade class... the year was 1988. My teacher, Ms. Meltzer, asked all the students to vote for who we wanted to be the next president. I do remember picking Jesse Jackson... out of all the pictures of the men who were running for president in 1988, he was the only one who looked like me. Then like all the little black children I wanted to be the first African American President. And now today 21 years later, I have the opportunity to watch a black man raise his right hand with his left hand placed on a bible to take the oath to be president of the United States of America...

1-19-09: Today is the celebration of Martin Luther King's birthday... so Wendy and I drove to The Reginald F. Lewis Museum of Maryland African American History & Culture... I have never heard the "I Have A Dream" speech in its entirety in Martin's own voice. I sat there and really listened to what the man had to say. In less than 24 hours Martin's dream that "one day this nation will rise up and live out the true meaning of its creed: We hold these truths to be self-evident, that all men are created equal," will be realized as we swear in the US' first black president. I just sat in awe as I took in our country's history.

1/19/09-1/20/09: In Washington, my cousin Arline Gibbs, who is well in her 80s stayed up waiting for us and let us stay with her until we needed to leave at 3:30am. It was so amazing to talk with her about the inauguration of Barack Obama; she had newspapers featuring our new president spread out on her coffee table and newspaper clippings of the event... After my cousin went upstairs to sleep I laid on her couch and drifted in and out of sleep... how could I sleep when in just a few hours I was going to witness history. My alarm went off at 3:15 and I bundled up. I packed my pockets with my hand warmers, Fig Newton's for snack, my bottled water, some cash for souvenirs, my camera, extra batteries, and my ID. This is it! I am about to see something people only dreamed and prayed for. My heart was pumping a little bit faster, the smile on my face was getting a little bit wider and the countdown began! We got to the Fort Totten Train Station, parked our car and stood online outside the station waiting for the doors to open at 4:00am. As the crowd was let in you could feel the energy. Everyone was smiling at each other, taking pictures of the train station... Like a can of sardines, we all packed on to the train intently listening for the announcer to tell us which stop we were at. Judiciary Square... at last we were in line... So, what do you do at 4:30 in the morning surrounded by thousands of other people waiting for history to happen... you laugh, tell jokes, find out where everyone is from and take lots and lots of pictures. It was 4:30am, about 20 degrees with a wind chill of ridiculously cold, on hour one of a 14 hour day of standing and I couldn't have been happier.

Live at the Inauguration

At about 8:30 the police opened the purple gates and we were able to go through the check point. We emptied our pockets, walked through metal detectors, and we ran to the very edge of the purple section gate. We just stood there with bright smiles on our faces. Imagine someone has a camera and tells you to say cheese and they are about to take your picture…, but they never take the picture. I had an eternal smile on my face that nothing was about to wipe away and so did everyone around me. The sun was finally out and the excitement was electric. I know I am leaving out so much of what happened that day, the people I met and so many stories I could tell, but 7 and a half hours after first getting on line on the cold morning of January 20th, Barack Obama stepped in front of Chief Justice Roberts with his wife Michelle by his side and he placed his left hand on the Lincoln Bible. Barack Obama raised his right hand and 34 seconds later he was and is our 44th president. The cheers were so loud and almost all the cheeks of the people around me were wet. It has been such a long journey but it feels good to end this writing knowing that Barack Obama is mine and your 44th President.

Historical Note

Embedded among the two million people who flocked Washington, D.C. on Inauguration Day were five members of the young adult ministry at Second Baptist Church. Ms. Jennifer Jones, Ms. Wendy Adi-Darko, Ms. Tiah Coley, Ms. Danielle Malloy, and Ms. Julie Jewels were there.

Prayer point: Father God, please show us how to love one another as you have loved us, in Jesus' name. Amen.

VOICES OF OUR YOUTH

Inspired by

The New York Daily News Children's Letters

Dear President Obama,

CONGRATULATIONS!!!!!!!

I was hoping that you would get elected as president. I was very happy that thousands of people came out to Grant Park. (Chicago, Illinois). I'm also happy that you're our first African American and 44th President of the USA. All those people out there at the inauguration were probably freezing, but the change has come. You can be an inspiration to all.

You decided to take the lead to mold this nation into your likings. I'm kind of sorry for John McCain for not being elected as president. Not to be rude…but his speeches weren't as good as yours, Mr. Obama. Mr. McCain speeches didn't have too much feeling. Mr. Obama's speeches had lots of feeling to it. When I heard your speech I just knew that you were going to be president.

I would love to have a sleepover with Sasha and Malia. Your wife is so beautiful, good choice Mr. Obama. I made a nickname for you…Obaga! Really my sister made it up. Have a nice time at the White House. You are really delightful, Obama. My family will also pray for you and your family. This is a poem I made up…Obama, Obama, you are the best. The Lord is there for you too.

When Martin Luther King was born there were slaves* and Martin tried his best to protect Black people so they won't get hurt. Back then, in the older days when Martin was a little boy he dreamed that all black and white children would get along and be friends, like now. When Martin Luther King Jr. was shot there was nothing to do but fight. Black people had to fight their own battles. They did a boycott and they didn't ride the buses.

In Obama's time, I think you can help us in a lot of ways. Just help the people in America. Don't let anyone convince you that you shouldn't help people, or stop you from doing your job. Please help this nation be a better place than before. Mr. Obama things you can help me on are making my school in Edison, NJ be better, so the teachers can teach me a lot or help me with my multiplications. I love you President Obama.

By Jaida Baptist, Age 9

Prayer Point: "Obama, you are the best. The Lord is there for you too." -Jaida B.

Jaida Baptist, age 9, was one of only two youngsters who submitted letters to President Obama for inclusion in the "Election Reflections" series. Her twin brother Jared also participated.

Dear Mr. President Barack Obama,

My name is Jared Baptist. I'm 9 years old and I am in the third grade. Let's stop talking about me now. Can you stop the war? You are the first African American president. I hope you help the world. You are going to be a great president for many people.

I watched the inauguration and I heard your speech. I also heard Mr. Joe Biden who is now the vice president. It doesn't matter about skin color, white people could vote for you too. Americans all over the world could vote for John McCain, but my family and I voted for you. I love the way you said your speech, it was AWESOME. I hope you are a helpful president and help everybody in the world to learn more from your family and really YOU. I know you are going to help people because you are a delightful president. You are smart and you can help the whole wide world in the universe. CHANGE IS COMING TO AMERICA by having a new president that's African American.

When Dr. Martin Luther King Jr. was born there was slavery* for the Black people and there were signs that said, "Whites only." Martin Luther King worked to stop that. Five years later he said his speech, "I HAVE A DREAM" then he died. When Barack Obama became president of the United States of America I know he would help me to do better in school so I can get my degree and a job.

By **Jared Baptist, Age 9**
2/3/2009 Edison, NJ

Jared Baptist, age 9, and his twin sister Jaida were the only two youngsters who submitted letters to President Obama for inclusion in the "Election Reflections" series.

Inspired by the New Jersey Star-Ledger Contest

WHAT BARACK OBAMA'S ELECTION MEANS TO ME

By: Annie Alexis Carty, Age 8

It started when I watched the INAUGURATION. I saw the first African American President. I saw Barack Obama! I saw about 2,000,000 people! They were there since morning, out in the freezing cold. It's better watching it in your house with popcorn. Even though you might not be able to hear as good, it's okay. Anyway, I heard the speech and the oath. I heard a beautiful benediction. Thank you, Jesus!

All of it touched my heart. I loved it! It was the first INAUGURATION I ever saw. Best of all… it set goals for me! I want to be a concert pianist, a president, and a bus driver. I know I can achieve those goals, and nothing is going to stop me because I can be anything I want to be. Yes I can! Now, this world can believe that blacks can be whatever they want to be.

At first, it was not fair… Once, Dinah White, a lady in my church, her uncle was walking on the sidewalk with his head hanging down. In those times black people would have to jump out of the way for white people. There were a couple of white folks a-walkin. He had his head down so he could not see them. They yelled at him! He tried to jump out of the way, but fell, and touched a white woman's foot. Then they hung him from a tree and killed him. You see, in those days, whites ruled over blacks. That was not fair.

Now, since a black man got in the White House, we can believe. If you put your mind to it, you can do it. Praise the Lord! Hallelujah! Thank you, Jesus!

January 24, 2009

Annie Alexis Carty read each story her mother Shauna Jamieson Carty reported for the "Election Reflections" series. She included her reaction to Mrs. Dinah White's story in her essay.

Historical Note

President Lincoln issued a proclamation in1862 thereby freeing some slaves. The 13th Amendment to the US Constitution ended slavery in 1865. Unfortunately, violence against blacks, forced segregation, and a denial of voting privileges and other civil rights give the casual observer the impression that blacks were still enslaved and that Rev. Dr. Martin Luther King Jr. was fighting for their liberation from slavery.

Reflections of a Wistful Journalist

By Shauna Jamieson Carty

The image of President-elect Obama, his wife, incoming First Lady Michelle, and their two daughters appearing on stage before billions moments before he gave his victory speech etched a permanent place of pride in many of our minds. This is a new pinnacle for the black man, whose image is broadcasted daily by the media as a criminal, deadbeat dad, and as being unpatriotic. Viewers needed only to watch the tears streaming down Jesse Jackson's face, and hear the jubilant shouts of praise as Rev. Dr. Martin Luther King, Jr.'s children celebrated in church, to be touched by the powerful emotions of this moment.

History will note that President Obama was an unlikely candidate to win the 2008 presidential election, but for starkly different reasons than his predecessor. If someone had been charting a timeline predicting America's history, President Obama taking office in 2009 hurls the nation's history light years forward. It wasn't supposed to happen yet.

This was the year of the woman. It was Senator Hillary Rodham Clinton's turn. Many believed the former First Lady was poised to become the first female president this year, succeeding her husband former President Bill Clinton eight years later in the White House. The Republican candidate, Senator John McCain, added a female vice presidential candidate to his ticket in the hopes of securing that pro-female vote. Unfortunately, Governor Sarah Palin failed to gain the public's confidence because she lacked Senator Clinton's political experience and track record in advocating for the American people.

Before he entered the White House, history will note that President Obama was an advocate for poor residents of Chicago. This brilliant man already earned historical note as the first black editor of the Harvard Law Review.

His multicultural background stirs immigrant pride in a country that in recent years has blamed many of its problems on immigrants. The fact that President Obama's father hailed from the continent of Africa redirects the media from its relentless portrayal of the unwanted immigrant. The fact that his parents blended two races in conceiving their son reinforces the fact that Rev. Dr. Martin Luther King Jr.'s dream that one day "little black boys and little black girls will be able to join hands with little white boys and little white girls…" has—to some extent—become a reality.

Yet, my favorite image of President Obama will be that of family man, shattering the stereotype of the promiscuous black man who won't take financial responsibility for his children. President Obama will be a real life example of international proportions, which was only preceded by the fictional image of Bill Cosby on the Cosby Show.

Yes, God bless America. May God guide and protect our incoming president and his family, in Jesus' name.

("Reflections of a Wistful Journalist" was not a part of the "Election Reflections" series although it was written during the same time period capturing the sentiments many people felt shortly after President Obama's election and inauguration.)

Photo Index and Sources

1. Mrs. Josephine Taylor Evans was photographed by Shauna Jamieson Carty.
2. Rev. James E. Moore, Sr. and *The New York Times* reporter Mr. Kevin Coyne were photographed by Shauna Jamieson Carty.
3. The group was photographed by Mrs. Delores Whitehead.
4. *The New York Times* photographer Mr. Timothy Ivy in action was photographed by Shauna Jamieson Carty.
5. Second Baptist Church, Roselle, New Jersey was photographed by Shauna Jamieson Carty.
6. Mrs. Dinah White and Mr. Duane White were photographed by Shauna Jamieson Carty.
7. Mrs. Evans and Mrs. Delores Whitehead were photographed by Shauna Jamieson Carty.
8. Mr. G.G. Woody provided the photograph of himself and his wife.
9. Mr. G.G. Woody and Ms. Leslie Woody were photographed by Shauna Jamieson Carty.
10. The group photo of Mr. G.G. Woody and Senator Robert Kennedy was provided by Mr. G.G. Woody.
11. Mr. and Mrs. McIntyre were photographed by Shauna Jamieson Carty.
12. Mr. and Mrs. Bragg provided the photograph of themselves.
13. Mr. Bragg provided the page from his high school yearbook.
14. Mrs. Bragg provided the page from her high school yearbook.
15. Mr. and Mrs. Thompson were photographed by Shauna Jamieson Carty.
16. Mrs. Marguerite White provided the photograph of her family.
17. Mrs. Williams and Mrs. Turner were photographed by Shauna Jamieson Carty.
18. The newspaper clipping showing Briggs Sign Shop was provided by Mrs. Marian Williams.
19. Ms. Jennifer Jones provided the photograph of her and Ms. Wendy Adi-Darko.
20. Ms. Jennifer Jones provided the photograph of herself in front of the monument.
21. Ms. Jennifer Jones provided the photograph of the crowd at the inauguration.
22. Ms. Jaida Baptist was photographed by Shauna Jamieson Carty.
23. Mr. Jared Baptist was photographed by Shauna Jamieson Carty.
24. Ms. Annie Carty was photographed by Shauna Jamieson Carty.